a visit to the LIBRARY

CHILDRENS PRESS™

CHICAGO

by Sylvia Root Tester

With sincere appreciation to the staff of GAIL BORDEN LIBRARY, Elgin, Illinois, for their cooperation in the photographing of this book.

And to the children who cooperated so patiently as we recorded their visit to the library on film.

Photography by PILOT PRODUCTIONS, INC.
  Dave Holmes, photographer
  Jay Kelly, lighting assistant
  Dean Garrison, director

Library of Congress Cataloging in Publication Data

Tester, Sylvia Root, 1939-
  A visit to the library.

  (Field trip series)
  Summary: A group of children visit a library, where they see a puppet show, listen to a story, and learn how to check out and take care of books.
  1. Libraries—Juvenile literature.   2. Books and reading—Juvenile literature.   [1. Libraries.   2. Books and reading]   I. Holmes, Dave, ill.   II. Title. III. Series.
Z665.5.T47   1985   027.62'5   84-12637
ISBN 0-516-01492-7

1 2 3 4 5 6 7 8 9 10 11 12 R 92 91 90 89 88 87 86

a visit to the LIBRARY

Created by The Child's World

Mrs. Johnson's class is at the library for a
visit. She gives each child a name tag.
Manuel pins his to his shirt just as a librarian comes to greet them.

"Welcome to the library," says the head librarian. "We will start your visit by going into a special room—a room just for children."

In the special room, the children gather
around another librarian. She smiles.
"I'm going to teach you a new song,"
she says.

Soon all the children are singing. They
clap along. The song makes them feel
happy.

After the singing, the children see a puppet show about children's books. A witch stars in it. She is so funny. The children laugh and laugh.

During the show, the librarian tells the children how they can borrow books. "You must take a paper home," she says. "Your parents must sign it. When you bring it back to the library, you will be given a card. Then you can borrow books."

The witch puppet holds up her library card. It has her name on it. It is covered with plastic.

"I want my own card," many of the children think.

The puppet show is over. The children
wave good-by to the funny witch.

Next, a book doctor talks to the children.
She shows them some sick books.

"A dog chewed this book" says the book
doctor. "It is hurt! I can't fix it!"

"Someone dropped this book in the
bathtub. It is drowned. I can't fix it either.

"Oh, look! Someone scribbled all over
this book. And I can't fix it."

"Be careful with books," the book doctor
says. "Don't let your pets play with them.
Don't let your little brothers and sisters get
them. Don't let the books get wet. Don't
tear the books either. Will you be careful?"

"Yes," everyone says.

The doctor shows them a book she can fix. A page is torn. She puts some special tape on the page.

Then the librarian reads a story to the class. The children like it! It's a funny story.

After the story, the children get to look at
all the things in the room. There are record
players and games.

There are story machines. Mrs. Garcia
starts one for some of the children. They
will see pictures and hear a story.

And there are puzzles. "We'll do the
puzzles," Manuel says. "They're fun!"

Next, Manuel stops to look at a big picture on the wall. He wants to see the computer, but Sandy is already looking at it. The names of all the books in the library are in the computer.

22

23

And there are lots of books. Everywhere there are books. Picture books. . .storybooks. . .books about dinosaurs. . .books about airplanes. . .books about bats. . . books about lions and tigers!

Jean finds a book about dolls. Jean already has a library card. She can check out her book.

Manuel doesn't have a card yet. "Pick a book, Manuel," the teacher says. "I'll check it out for you." Finally, Manuel chooses a book about Mexico. His uncle lives in Mexico.

The teacher gives Manuel a paper. "Take this home and get it signed," she tells Manuel. "Then you may check out books."

"I will," says Manuel.

Soon it is time for the visit to end.

"Good-by, Manuel," says a librarian.

"Good-by," says Manuel. "But I'll be back. I'm going to read all the books in the library. Every one!"

"Good," the librarian says. "We'll look for you, Manuel. Don't forget to say, 'Hi,' next time you come."

"I won't," Manuel says.

He's glad he has a friend at the library. It
is such a happy place to visit.
He hurries to the waiting bus.